20 best
birthday cake
recipes for kids

Houghton Mifflin Harcourt
Boston • New York • 2013

Copyright © 2013 by General Mills, Minneapolis, Minnesota. All rights reserved.

For information about permission to reproduce selections from this book, write to Permissions, Houghton Mifflin Harcourt Publishing Company, 215 Park Avenue South, New York, New York 10003.

www.hmhco.com

Cover photo: Trix Cereal Crunch Cake (page 27)

General Mills
Food Content and Relationship Marketing Director: Geoff Johnson
Food Content Marketing Manager: Susan Klobuchar
Senior Editor: Grace Wells
Kitchen Manager: Ann Stuart
Recipe Development and Testing: Betty Crocker Kitchens
Photography: General Mills Photography Studios and Image Library

Houghton Mifflin Harcourt
Publisher: Natalie Chapman
Editorial Director: Cindy Kitchel
Executive Editor: Anne Ficklen
Associate Editor: Heather Dabah
Managing Editor: Rebecca Springer
Production Editor: Kristi Hart
Cover Design: Chrissy Kurpeski
Book Design: Tai Blanche

ISBN 978-0-544-31464-1
Printed in the United States of America

The Betty Crocker Kitchens seal guarantees success in your kitchen. Every recipe has been tested in America's Most Trusted Kitchens™ to meet our high standards of reliability, easy preparation and great taste.

FIND MORE GREAT IDEAS AT
BettyCrocker.com

Dear Friends,

This new collection of colorful mini books has been put together with you in mind because we know that you love great recipes and enjoy cooking and baking but have a busy lifestyle. So every little book in the series contains just 20 recipes for you to treasure and enjoy. Plus, each book is a single subject designed in a bite-size format just for you—it's easy to use and is filled with favorite recipes from the Betty Crocker Kitchens!

All of the books are conveniently divided into short chapters so you can quickly find what you're looking for, and the beautiful photos throughout are sure to entice you into making the delicious recipes. In the series, you'll discover a fabulous array of recipes to spark your interest—from cookies, cupcakes and birthday cakes to party ideas for a variety of occasions. There's grilled foods, potluck favorites and even gluten-free recipes too.

You'll love the variety in these mini books—so pick one or choose them all for your cooking pleasure.

Enjoy and happy cooking!

Sincerely,

Betty Crocker

contents

Favorite Things
Roller Coaster Cake • 6
Automobile Cake • 7
Cell Phone Cake • 8
Robot Cake • 10
Soccer Ball Cake • 12
Monster Cake • 13
Space Shuttle Cake • 14

Party Themes
Sports Party Cake • 16
Slumber Party Cake • 17
Pirate Cake • 18
Electric Guitar Cake • 20
Poppin' Up Happy Birthday Cake • 22
Gum Ball Machine Cake • 24

Just for Fun
"Let's Party" Cake • 25
Spiral Candle Cake • 26
Trix Cereal Crunch Cake • 27
Butterfly Cake • 28
Confetti Birthday Cake • 30
Rainbow Angel Cake • 31
Chocolate Lover's Dream Cake • 32

Metric Conversion Guide • 34
Recipe Testing and Calculating Nutrition Information • 35

Favorite Things

Roller Coaster Cake

Prep Time: 40 Minutes • **Start to Finish:** 2 Hours 10 Minutes • Makes 24 servings

Bring the fun of an amusement park to your party with a sheet cake decorated to look like a roller coaster ride!

1 Heat oven to 350°F (325°F for dark or nonstick pan). Spray bottom only of 15 x 10 x 1-inch pan with baking spray with flour.

2 Make cake batter as directed on box. Pour into pan. Bake 20 to 26 minutes (22 to 29 minutes for dark or nonstick pan) or until toothpick inserted in center comes out clean. Cool completely, about 1 hour.

3 Frost cake with vanilla frosting. With toothpick, lightly draw shape of roller coaster on cake (see photo). Squeeze drops of food color in several places on frosting above roller coaster outline; use knife to swirl into frosting for sky.

4 Tear or cut fruit snack in half lengthwise; place strips on cake to make track of roller coaster. Add pretzels for supports. Add fruit slice candies just above track for cars; place 2 brown baking bits under each car for wheels.

5 In small microwavable bowl, microwave chocolate frosting uncovered on Medium (50%) 15 seconds; stir. Dip top third of each candy wafer into melted frosting; top with sprinkles for hair. Place 1 wafer "face" on top of each car.

6 Place remaining melted frosting in small resealable food-storage plastic bag; seal bag. Cut small tip off 1 corner of bag. Pipe dot of frosting on each red baking bit; attach to wafers for mouths. Add licorice candies on both sides of each wafer candy for arms. Store loosely covered.

Cake

1 box Betty Crocker® SuperMoist® butter recipe yellow cake mix

Water, butter and eggs called for on cake mix box

Frosting and Decorations

1 container (12 oz) Betty Crocker Whipped vanilla frosting

Blue food color

1 roll Betty Crocker Fruit by the Foot® chewy fruit snack (from 4.5-oz box)

21 thin pretzel sticks

3 fruit slice candies (flat)

6 miniature brown candy-coated semisweet chocolate baking bits

1 tablespoon Betty Crocker Rich & Creamy chocolate frosting

3 thin pink candy wafers (1 inch diameter)

½ teaspoon chocolate candy sprinkles

3 miniature red candy-coated semisweet chocolate baking bits

6 oblong (1 inch) pink candy-coated licorice pieces

1 Serving (Cake and Frosting Only): Calories 160; Total Fat 7g (Saturated Fat 3g, Trans Fat 1g); Cholesterol 35mg; Sodium 170mg; Total Carbohydrate 24g (Dietary Fiber 0g); Protein 1g **Exchanges:** ½ Starch, 1 Other Carbohydrate, 1½ Fat **Carbohydrate Choices:** 1½

Automobile Cake

Prep Time: 1 Hour 5 Minutes • **Start to Finish:** 4 Hours • Makes 12 servings

Cake
2 cups Gold Medal® all-purpose flour
1 cup granulated sugar
3 teaspoons baking powder
½ teaspoon salt
¼ cup butter, softened
¼ cup shortening
¾ cup milk
1 teaspoon vanilla
2 eggs

Frosting
⅔ cup butter, softened
5½ cups powdered sugar
2 teaspoons vanilla
About 3 tablespoons milk
Desired food color

Decorations
Tray or cardboard (13 x 9½ inches), covered with wrapping paper and plastic food wrap, or foil
4 creme-filled chocolate sandwich cookies
1 tube (.68 oz) black or brown decorating gel
Black and white licorice beans
1 white and 2 red gum balls
Silver nonpareils

1 Heat oven to 300°F. Grease 2 (9 x 5-inch) loaf pans with shortening; lightly flour. In large bowl, beat all cake ingredients with electric mixer on medium speed 30 seconds, scraping bowl constantly. Beat on high speed 2 minutes, scraping bowl occasionally. Divide batter evenly between pans.

2 Bake 40 to 45 minutes or until toothpick inserted in center comes out clean. Cool 10 minutes; remove from pans to cooling racks. Cool completely, about 1 hour.

3 Cut and remove 3-inch piece from end of 1 loaf; discard or save for another use. Freeze remaining piece uncovered about 1 hour for easier frosting.

4 In large bowl, beat ⅔ cup butter and the powdered sugar with electric mixer on medium speed until smooth. Gradually beat in 2 teaspoons vanilla and 2 tablespoons of the milk, adding more milk if necessary for spreading consistency. Reserve ½ cup frosting in small bowl. Tint remaining frosting with food color.

5 Place whole loaf on tray. Frost top with ⅓ cup of the colored frosting. Top with cut piece of loaf, positioning as shown in photo; trim front and back as desired to resemble car front and back. Attach cookies with small amount of frosting for wheels. Draw outline of windows with sharp knife. Frost windows and hubcaps with reserved white frosting. Frost sides and top of car with remaining colored frosting, building up around wheels for fenders.

6 Using decorating gel, outline windows, hood, doors and bumpers. Attach licorice beans for grille, door handles and signal lights. Cut gum balls in half; attach for headlights and taillights. Make spoke markings on wheel with knife. Press 1 silver nonpareil in center of each wheel. Attach silver nonpareils for hood ornament if desired. Remove nonpareils before serving cake.

1 Serving: Calories 640; Total Fat 23g (Saturated Fat 11g, Trans Fat 1.5g); Cholesterol 75mg; Sodium 400mg; Total Carbohydrate 102g (Dietary Fiber 1g); Protein 4g **Exchanges:** 1½ Starch, 5½ Other Carbohydrate, 4½ Fat **Carbohydrate Choices:** 7

Cell Phone Cake

Prep Time: 35 Minutes • **Start to Finish:** 2 Hours 50 Minutes • Makes 15 servings

Cake

1 box Betty Crocker SuperMoist white cake mix

Water, vegetable oil and egg whites called for on cake mix box

Tray or cardboard (18 x 16 inches), covered with wrapping paper and plastic food wrap or foil

Frosting and Decorations

1½ containers (1 lb each) Betty Crocker Rich & Creamy creamy white frosting

Pink paste or gel food color

Decorating bag with tips

12 white candy-coated chewing gum squares

1 package (3.2 oz) marshmallow flowers

3 oval licorice candies

1 candy straw

There's no need to put in a call to a baker for your teen girl's birthday. Ring in the big day with a clever homemade cake!

1 Heat oven to 350°F (325°F for dark or nonstick pan). Spray bottom only of 13 x 9-inch pan with baking spray with flour. Make and bake cake mix as directed on box for 13 x 9-inch pan. Cool 10 minutes; remove from pan to cooling rack. Cool completely, about 1 hour.

2 Cut 1¼-inch strip from each long side of cake. Trim each corner of cake to round off, making cell phone shape as shown in diagrams 1 and 2. (Discard pieces trimmed from cake or reserve for another use.) Place cake on tray as shown in diagram 3. Freeze 1 hour.

3 Divide 1 container of white frosting in half (about ¾ cup each). Place half of frosting in small bowl. Stir food color into half of frosting to tint pink. Frost bottom half of cake with pink frosting. Frost top half of cake with white frosting.

4 From ½ container of frosting, reserve about 2 tablespoons white frosting in small bowl. In another small bowl, tint about ¼ cup of the frosting pink. Onto center of white-frosted half of cake, spread some of the pink frosting in square shape for message screen. Place remaining pink frosting in decorating bag with writing tip. Pipe pink frosting along edge of white-frosted cake. Arrange gum on cake for number buttons; pipe on numbers with pink frosting.

5 With reserved white frosting, pipe desired message on message screen. Add marshmallow flowers and licorice candies. Add candy straw for antenna. Store loosely covered.

1 Serving (Cake and Frosting Only): Calories 340; **Total Fat** 13g (Saturated Fat 2.5g; Trans Fat 2.5g); Cholesterol 0mg; Sodium 320mg; Total Carbohydrate 54g (Dietary Fiber 0g); Protein 2g **Exchanges:** 1 Starch, 2½ Other Carbohydrate, 2½ Fat **Carbohydrate Choices:** 3½

Tip Instead of using a decorating bag and tip, place the frosting in a resealable food-storage plastic bag, cut a tiny tip off one corner and use to pipe the frosting. Use different bags for different colors.

Cutting and Assembling Cell Phone Cake

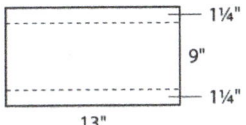

1. Cut 1¼-inch strip from each long side of cake.

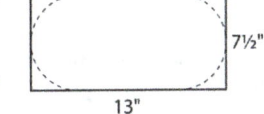

2. Trim each corner of cake to round off, making cell phone shape.

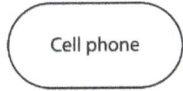

3. Place cake on tray.

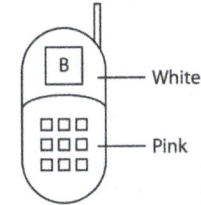

4. Frost top half of cake with white frosting and bottom half with pink frosting.

Favorite Things

Robot Cake

Prep Time: 1 Hour 45 Minutes • **Start to Finish:** 4 Hours 25 Minutes • Makes 12 servings

Cake

- 1 box Betty Crocker SuperMoist yellow cake mix
- Water, vegetable oil and eggs called for on cake mix box
- Tray or cardboard (20 x 15 inches), covered with wrapping paper and plastic food wrap or foil

Frosting and Decorations

- 1½ containers (1 lb each) Betty Crocker Rich & Creamy vanilla frosting
- Black food color
- Blue food color
- 2 colorful licorice twists (7 inch)
- 2 large black gumdrops
- 2 soft fruit ring candies
- 2 blue candy-coated chocolate candies
- 3 pull-apart red (cherry) licorice twists
- 20 candy-coated chocolate candies (any color)
- 1 roll Betty Crocker Fruit by the Foot chewy fruit snack (any variety from 4.5-oz box)
- 6 thin chocolate wafer cookies

Create a fun cake that's all decked out with Fruit by the Foot chewy snack and a delightful assortment of kids' candies.

1 Heat oven to 350°F (325°F for dark or nonstick pan). Grease or spray bottom and sides of 13 x 9-inch pan. Make and bake cake as directed on box for 13 x 9-inch pan. Cool 10 minutes; remove from pan to cooling rack. Cool completely, about 1 hour. Refrigerate or freeze cake 1 hour or until firm.

2 Tint frosting with black and blue food colors to make desired gray color. Using serrated knife, cut rounded top off cake to level surface; place cake cut side down on work surface. Cut cake as shown in diagram 1. On tray, arrange cake pieces as shown in diagram 2, attaching to tray with small amount of frosting. Spread thin layer of frosting over top and sides to seal in crumbs. Refrigerate or freeze cake 30 to 60 minutes to set frosting.

3 Frost entire cake with remaining frosting. Cut 1 colorful licorice twist into 2 (1-inch) pieces. Carefully insert licorice pieces between head and body.

4 Cut remaining colorful licorice twist in half. Using scissors, make several cuts in 1 end of each licorice piece to form antennae. Insert licorice pieces, antennae ends up, into top of head. Insert gumdrops in sides of head for ears. Arrange fruit rings on head for eyes; use 2 blue candy-coated chocolate candies for pupils. Separate 1 pull-apart red licorice twist into single strands. Trim 1 strand to 3 inches; place on head for mouth. Use remaining strands to decorate base of robot as desired, trimming to fit.

5 Tie a knot in each remaining pull-apart red licorice twist. Insert knotted licorice twists in each side of body for arms. To decorate robot body, arrange 20 candy-coated chocolate candies in desired pattern on body. Use fruit snack to form border around candy design, trimming to fit. For wheels, insert chocolate wafer cookies in base of cake. Store loosely covered.

1 Serving (Cake and Frosting Only): Calories 430; Total Fat 19g (Saturated Fat 4g, Trans Fat 3.5g); Cholesterol 50mg; Sodium 360mg; Total Carbohydrate 65g (Dietary Fiber 0g); Protein 2g **Exchanges:** 1 Starch, 3½ Other Carbohydrate, 3½ Fat **Carbohydrate Choices:** 4

Cutting and Assembling Robot Cake

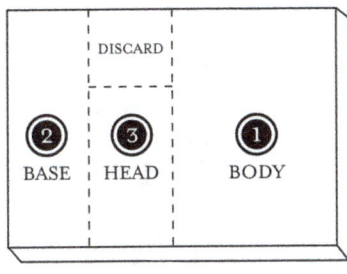
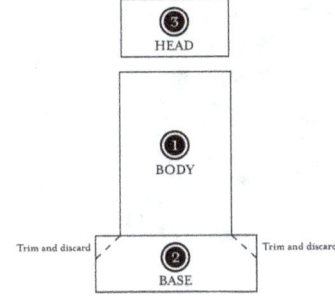

1. Cut cake for body, base and head.

2. Arrange pieces on tray to form robot.

Soccer Ball Cake

Prep Time: 40 Minutes • **Start to Finish:** 2 Hours 55 Minutes • Makes 12 servings

Is there a soccer player having a birthday? Invite the whole team to the party! This cake is easy to make and serves 12.

1 Heat oven to 350°F (325°F for dark or nonstick pan). Spray bottom only of 13 x 9-inch pan with baking spray with flour. Grease 1-quart ovenproof glass bowl with shortening; coat with flour (do not use baking spray).

2 Make cake batter as directed on box. Pour 1⅓ cups batter into 1-quart bowl and remaining batter into 13 x 9-inch pan.

3 Bake 13 x 9-inch pan 21 to 26 minutes (23 to 30 minutes for dark or nonstick) and 1-quart bowl 26 to 31 minutes or until toothpick inserted in center comes out clean. Cool 10 minutes; remove from pan and bowl to cooling racks (place cake from bowl with rounded side up). Cool completely, about 30 minutes.

4 Cut off uneven bottom of cake from bowl so it will stand flat. Freeze cakes 1 hour.

5 On tray, place 13 x 9-inch cake bottom side up. Stir food color into 1½ cups of the white frosting; spread over cake.

6 Spread remaining ½ cup white frosting over rounded side of other cake for soccer ball. Place ball on green field. Use black decorating icing to create soccer ball design. Use green decorating icing to make tufts of grass. Store loosely covered.

Cake

1 box Betty Crocker SuperMoist yellow cake mix

Water, vegetable oil and eggs called for on cake mix box

Tray or cardboard (18 x 16 inches), covered with wrapping paper and plastic food wrap or foil

Frosting and Decoration

3 drops green liquid food color

2 cups Betty Crocker Rich & Creamy creamy white frosting (from 2 containers, 1 lb each)

Black decorating icing (from 4.25-oz tube)

Green decorating icing (from 4.25-oz tube)

1 Serving (Cake and Frosting Only): Calories 420; Total Fat 18g (Saturated Fat 4g, Trans Fat 2.5g); Cholesterol 55mg; Sodium 370mg; Total Carbohydrate 61g (Dietary Fiber 0g); Protein 2g **Exchanges:** ½ Starch, 3½ Other Carbohydrate, 3½ Fat **Carbohydrate Choices:** 4

Tip If volleyball is your sport, just decorate the ball to resemble a volleyball.

Monster Cake

Prep Time: 45 Minutes • **Start to Finish:** 2 Hours • Makes 12 servings

Enjoy this creatively decorated monster cake—change colors and candy as desired to suit your party theme.

1 Heat oven to 350°F (325°F for dark or nonstick pan). Make and bake cake as directed on box for 13 x 9-inch pan. Cool 10 minutes; remove from pan to cooling rack. Cool completely, about 1 hour.

2 Place cake bottom side up on large platter or foil-covered cookie sheet. Remove 2 tablespoons of white frosting from container; set aside. Remove one-third of the frosting (about ½ cup) to small bowl. Tint black; set aside. Tint remaining frosting neon green. Frost sides and top of cake with neon green frosting.

3 Using photo as a guide, use decorating icing with a round tip to outline hair. Add licorice pieces for eyebrows. Use reserved white frosting to form eyes. Use icing to outline remaining facial features. Spread black frosting within the outlines to fill in the hair. Store loosely covered.

1 box Betty Crocker SuperMoist chocolate fudge cake mix

Water, vegetable oil and eggs called for on cake mix box

1 container (1 lb) Betty Crocker Rich & Creamy creamy white frosting

Black food color

Neon green food color

Black decorating icing (from 4.25-oz tube)

2 pieces black string licorice (5 to 6 inch)

1 Serving: Calories 380; Total Fat 17g (Saturated Fat 3.5g; Trans Fat 2g); Cholesterol 55mg; Sodium 410mg; Total Carbohydrate 54g (Dietary Fiber 0g); Protein 3g **Exchanges:** 1 Starch, 2½ Other Carbohydrate, 3½ Fat **Carbohydrate Choices:** 3½

Tip Create an attractive display by covering a piece of sturdy cardboard with wrapping paper, then plastic food wrap. Stretch and secure it with tape. Or cover the cardboard with foil or cooking parchment paper.

Space Shuttle Cake

Prep Time: 1 Hour • **Start to Finish:** 4 Hours 25 Minutes • Makes 15 servings

Cake

1 box Betty Crocker SuperMoist yellow cake mix

Water, vegetable oil and eggs called for on cake mix box

Tray or cardboard (17 x 12 inches), covered with wrapping paper and plastic food wrap or foil

Frosting and Decorations

2 containers (1 lb each) Betty Crocker Rich & Creamy vanilla frosting

Red string licorice

Red and blue miniature candy-coated chocolate baking bits

2 red gumdrop stars

3 small candy stars

6 soft red round candies

1 tube (0.68 oz) black decorating gel

3 candles

Give your birthday party a perfect send-off with this fun cake.

1 Heat oven to 350°F (325°F for dark or nonstick pan). Grease or spray bottom and sides of 13 x 9-inch pan. Make and bake cake as directed on box for 13 x 9-inch pan. Cool 10 minutes; remove from pan to cooling rack. Cool completely, about 1 hour. Refrigerate or freeze cake 1 hour or until firm.

2 Using serrated knife, cut rounded dome from top of cake to make flat surface; place cake cut side down on work surface. Cut cake as shown in diagram 1.

3 On tray, place cake piece 1. Arrange pieces 2, 3 and 4 as shown in diagram 2, trimming to fit, standing up piece 3 for top fin. Trim point of piece 2 for nose of shuttle. Attach each piece with a small amount of frosting.

4 Spread thin layer of frosting over top and sides to seal in crumbs. Freeze cake 30 to 45 minutes to set frosting. Add final coat of frosting to cake, using up remaining frosting.

5 Use licorice to make diagonal lines across nose of shuttle and to outline top fin. Use baking bits to outline tip, wings and back of shuttle. Add large and small stars to wings and back; add round candies to both sides of fin. Write "USA" or another message on top of fin with decorating gel. Insert candles at end of shuttle. If desired, just before serving, light candles for "liftoff." Store loosely covered.

1 Serving (Cake and Frosting Only): Calories 410; Total Fat 17g (Saturated Fat 3.5g, Trans Fat 3.5g); Cholesterol 40mg; Sodium 320mg; Total Carbohydrate 62g (Dietary Fiber 0g); Protein 1g **Exchanges:** ½ Starch, 3½ Other Carbohydrate, 3½ Fat **Carbohydrate Choices:** 4

Tip Place strips of waxed paper under corners of unfrosted cake pieces. After frosting, just remove waxed-paper strips. No cleanup needed!

Cutting and Assembling Space Shuttle Cake

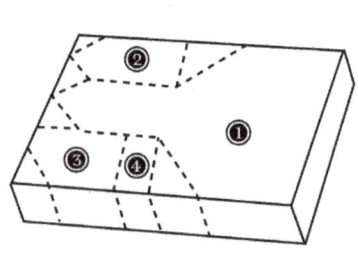

1. Cut cake to form pieces of space shuttle.

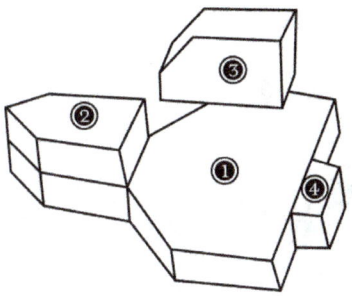

2. Arrange pieces on tray to form space shuttle.

Favorite Things · **15**

Party Themes

Sports Party Cake

Prep Time: 35 Minutes • **Start to Finish:** 4 Hours 15 Minutes • Makes 15 servings

1 box Betty Crocker SuperMoist cake mix (any flavor*)

Water, vegetable oil and eggs called for on cake mix box

Tray or cardboard (15 x 12 inches), covered with wrapping paper and plastic food wrap or foil

1½ containers (12 oz each) Betty Crocker Whipped fluffy white frosting

Food colors

Kids that are into sports will love having this for a birthday cake—you can vary the colors to suit the child and whatever sport that they enjoy.

1 Heat oven to 350°F (325°F for dark or nonstick pan). Spray bottom only of 13 x 9-inch pan with baking spray with flour.

2 Make and bake cake as directed on box for 13 x 9-inch pan. Cool 10 minutes; remove from pan to cooling rack. Cool completely, about 1 hour. Refrigerate or freeze cake 30 to 60 minutes or until firm.

3 Meanwhile, tint 2¼ cups of the frosting with food color as desired for your choice of color. Tint ½ cup frosting as desired for team name and numbers. Using serrated knife, cut rounded top off cake to level surface; place cake cut side down on work surface.

4 Place short side of cake toward you. Poke toothpick in cake at a point 4 inches from top and 1 inch from outside edge, on both sides. Poke toothpick in cake at bottom, 1 inch from outside edge, on both sides. Cut 1 x 8-inch piece (marked with toothpicks) from outer edge of each side. Cut each piece in half crosswise, forming 4 (1 x 4-inch) pieces. Cut neck hole from top of cake.

5 On tray, place largest piece of cake. Using small amount of jersey-colored frosting, attach 2 small rectangular pieces on each side of top of cake to lengthen sleeves. Spread with a thin layer of frosting to seal in crumbs. Refrigerate or freeze cake 30 to 60 minutes to set frosting.

6 Frost entire cake with jersey-colored frosting. Pipe other color frosting onto cake to create team name, numbers and shirt trim. Store loosely covered.

1 Serving: Calories 340; Total Fat 16g (Saturated Fat 4g, Trans Fat 2g); Cholesterol 40mg; Sodium 250mg; Total Carbohydrate 45g (Dietary Fiber 0g); Protein 2g **Exchanges:** 1 Starch, 2 Other Carbohydrate, 3 Fat **Carbohydrate Choices:** 3

*For all chocolate and devil's food cake mixes, use only 1 cup of the water.

Slumber Party Cake

Prep Time: 30 Minutes • **Start to Finish:** 2 Hours 20 Minutes • Makes 12 servings

Next time your kids have a sleepover birthday with friends, surprise them with this fun cake.

1 Heat oven to 350°F (325°F for dark or nonstick pan). Grease or spray bottom only of 13 x 9-inch pan. Make and bake cake mix as directed on box for 13 x 9-inch pan. Cool 10 minutes; remove from pan to cooling rack. Cool completely, about 1 hour.

2 Starting at short side of cake, frost one-third of cake with yellow cupcake icing for sheet. Place flattened marshmallows on sheet for pillows; place cookies on top of pillows for faces.

3 Frost remaining cake and portion of sandwich cookies with green cupcake icing for blanket, leaving top portion of cookie unfrosted for faces. Pipe hair and faces onto cookies with decorating icing. Using star tip, outline blanket with decorating icing. Sprinkle with confetti decors. Store loosely covered.

Cake
1 box Betty Crocker SuperMoist white cake mix

Water, vegetable oil and egg whites called for on cake mix box

Frosting and Decorations
1 can (8.4 oz) yellow cupcake icing

5 large marshmallows, flattened

5 creme-filled peanut butter sandwich cookies

1 can (8.4 oz) green cupcake icing

Decorating icing (any colors)

1 container confetti decorating decors

1 Serving: Calories 290; Total Fat 12g (Saturated Fat 3g, Trans Fat 1g); Cholesterol 0mg; Sodium 300mg; Total Carbohydrate 44g (Dietary Fiber 0g); Protein 2g **Exchanges:** 1 Starch, 2 Other Carbohydrate, 2 Fat **Carbohydrate Choices:** 3

Tip For convenience, substitute 1 container (1 lb) Betty Crocker Rich & Creamy vanilla frosting for the cupcake icings. Spoon about one-third of the frosting into a small bowl and tint with yellow food color. Place remaining frosting in another small bowl and tint with green food color. Instead of piping a border of icing on the blanket, arrange small decorative candies around the edge.

Pirate Cake

Prep Time: 30 Minutes • **Start to Finish:** 3 Hours 10 Minutes • Makes 12 servings

Cake

1 box Betty Crocker SuperMoist cake mix (any flavor)

Water, vegetable oil and eggs called for on cake mix box

Tray or cardboard (15 x 12 inches), covered with wrapping paper and plastic wrap or foil

Frosting and Decorations

2/3 cup Betty Crocker Rich & Creamy chocolate frosting (from 1-lb container)

1 container (1 lb) Betty Crocker Rich & Creamy vanilla frosting

1 chocolate-covered mint patty

1 large marshmallow, cut in half

1 blue gum ball or candy-coated chocolate candy

1 yellow ring-shaped hard candy

1 roll Betty Crocker Fruit by the Foot strawberry or other red chewy fruit snack (from 4.5-oz box)

1 black licorice rope

2 pieces square-shaped candy-coated gum

Chocolate candy sprinkles

1 Heat oven to 350°F (325°F for dark or nonstick pans). Grease bottoms and sides of 1 (8-inch) and 1 (9-inch) round cake pan with shortening or cooking spray. Make cake mix as directed on box. Divide batter evenly between pans.

2 Bake as directed. Cool 10 minutes; remove from pans to cooling racks. Cool completely, about 1 hour.

3 Using serrated knife, cut 9-inch cake in half. One half will form body of pirate. From other half, cut hat shape and ears as shown in diagram 1. Cut about a 1-inch edge off one side of 8-inch cake as shown in diagram 2 (flat edge will be top of pirate's head); cut nose from cut-off edge piece. On tray, place cake pieces as shown in diagram 3, using small amount of frosting to attach nose and ears. Cover; freeze cake 1 hour or until firm.

4 Reserve 2 teaspoons chocolate frosting in small bowl. Frost hat with remaining chocolate frosting. Mix 2/3 cup of the vanilla frosting with reserved chocolate frosting. With tinted vanilla frosting, frost head, ears and nose of pirate. Add mint patty for eye patch, marshmallow slice and gum ball for eye, and ring-shaped candy for earring.

5 Frost body with remaining vanilla frosting. Cut fruit snack into shapes for shirt stripes, mouth and strap for eye patch; place on cake. Cut licorice to fit hat. Add gum for teeth and candy sprinkles for whiskers. Store loosely covered at room temperature.

1 Serving Frosted Cake (Undecorated): Calories 430; Total Fat 19g (Saturated Fat 5g, Trans Fat 3.5g); Cholesterol 55mg; Sodium 370mg; Total Carbohydrate 62g (Dietary Fiber 0g); Protein 3g **Exchanges:** 1 Starch, 3 Other Carbohydrate, 3½ Fat **Carbohydrate Choices:** 4

Tip Cake pieces are frozen before decorating since cold cakes are easier to frost.

Cutting and Assembling Pirate Cake

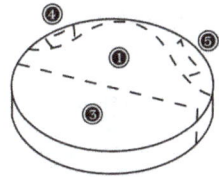

1. Cut 9-inch cake in half, then cut hat and ears.

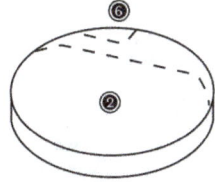

2. Cut 8-inch cake for the face and nose.

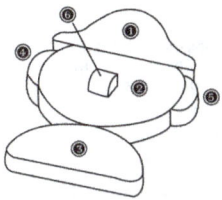

3. Arrange pieces on tray to form pirate.

Electric Guitar Cake

Prep Time: 1 Hour 30 Minutes • **Start to Finish:** 5 Hours • Makes 12 servings

Cake

- 1 box Betty Crocker SuperMoist yellow or devil's food cake mix
- 1 cup water
- ½ cup vegetable oil
- 3 eggs
- Tray or cardboard (19 x 11 inches), covered with wrapping paper and plastic food wrap or foil

Frosting and Decorations

- 1¼ cups Betty Crocker Rich & Creamy chocolate frosting (from 1-lb container)
- Black food color
- 2¾ cups Betty Crocker Rich & Creamy vanilla frosting (from 2 (1-lb) containers)
- Desired food color for guitar
- 4 pieces black licorice coil, uncoiled, or string licorice
- 4 small chewy fruit candies in desired color
- 6 chewy fruit-flavored gumdrops (not sugar coated) in desired color
- 2 candy-coated tropical fruit candies in desired color

Here is the perfect birthday party cake for a young music lover. Vary the colors and candies to suit your taste.

1 Heat oven to 350°F (325°F for dark or nonstick pan). Grease or spray bottom and sides of 13 x 9-inch pan. In large bowl, beat cake mix, water, oil and eggs with electric mixer on low speed 30 seconds, then on medium speed 2 minutes, scraping bowl occasionally. Pour into pan. Bake as directed on box for 13 x 9-inch pan. Cool 10 minutes; remove from pan to cooling rack. Cool completely, about 1 hour. Refrigerate or freeze cake 30 to 60 minutes or until firm.

2 Meanwhile, in medium bowl, mix chocolate frosting and black food color to make black frosting. In small bowl, mix ⅓ cup of the vanilla frosting and enough black food color to make gray frosting. Place gray frosting and ⅔ cup white vanilla frosting in separate resealable food-storage plastic bags; seal bags. Cut small tip off 1 corner of each bag. In another medium bowl, mix remaining vanilla frosting and desired food color to make guitar color.

3 Using serrated knife, cut rounded top off cake to level surface; place cake cut side down on work surface. Cut cake as shown in diagram 1. Place cake pieces on tray as shown in diagram 2, attaching to tray with small amount of frosting.

4 Spread thin layer of guitar frosting over top and sides of guitar body to seal in crumbs. Spread thin layer of black frosting over top and sides of guitar neck and headstock. Refrigerate or freeze cake 30 to 60 minutes to set frosting.

5 Frost entire cake with same colors. If desired, place remaining black frosting in resealable food-storage plastic bag and cut small tip off 1 corner of bag to pipe frosting. To extend guitar neck 1 to 2 inches onto body of guitar, pipe and fill in neck with black frosting. With white vanilla frosting, pipe and fill in contrasting design on body of guitar. On white design, pipe black rectangle about 1 inch from end of neck to create pickup. With gray frosting, pipe on frets, bridge and any additional accents as desired. For strings, add black licorice. Add small fruit candies at ends of strings. For tuning pegs, add gumdrops. For buttons on body, add tropical fruit candies. Store loosely covered.

1 Serving (Cake and Frosting Only): Calories 460; Total Fat 19g (Saturated Fat 4.5g, Trans Fat 4g); Cholesterol 40mg; Sodium 380mg; Total Carbohydrate 68g (Dietary Fiber 0g); Protein 2g **Exchanges:** 1 Starch, 3½ Other Carbohydrate, 3½ Fat **Carbohydrate Choices:** 4½

Cutting and Assembling Electric Guitar Cake

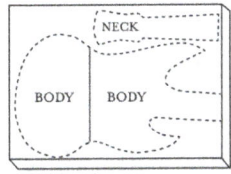 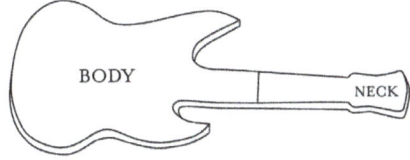

1. Cut cake for body and neck.

2. Arrange pieces on tray for electric guitar.

Poppin' Up Happy Birthday Cake

Prep Time: 35 Minutes • **Start to Finish:** 2 Hours 50 Minutes • Makes 15 servings

1 box Betty Crocker SuperMoist yellow cake mix

Water, vegetable oil and eggs called for on cake mix box

2 containers (1 lb each) Betty Crocker Rich & Creamy creamy white frosting

Tray or cardboard (24 x 16 inches), covered with wrapping paper and plastic food wrap or foil

Red pull-and-peel licorice

¼ bar (4-oz size) white chocolate

Blue decorating icing (from 4.25-oz tube)

2 cups popped microwave kettle corn popcorn

Savory popcorn and sweet cake come together in a unique cake appealing to both old and young alike!

1 Heat oven to 350°F (325°F for dark or nonstick pan). Spray bottom and side of 8-inch round cake pan with baking spray with flour. Grease and flour bottom and sides of 11 x 7-inch glass baking dish (do not use baking spray). Make cake batter as directed on box. Pour 1⅓ cups batter into 8-inch round pan and remaining batter into 11 x 7-inch baking dish.

2 Bake 8-inch pan 23 to 28 minutes (dark or nonstick 8-inch pan 26 to 33 minutes) and 11 x 7-inch dish 34 to 38 minutes or until toothpick inserted in center comes out clean. Cool 10 minutes; remove from pan and baking dish to cooling racks. Cool completely, about 30 minutes.

3 Cut 8-inch round cake crosswise in half. Spread 2 tablespoons frosting over top of 1 cake piece. Top with second cake piece.

4 Cut wedge shape from each long side of 11 x 7-inch cake so cake is 4 inches wide at one end and 7 inches wide at other end (see diagram 1). On tray, place larger cake piece with 4-inch end at one end of tray. Place stacked rounded cake at 7-inch end of cake on tray (see diagram 2) for kettle corn. Freeze cake 1 hour before frosting to reduce crumbs.

5 Spread desired amount of remaining frosting over entire cake. Peel 5 sections of licorice apart; arrange lengthwise on popcorn bag.

6 Place white chocolate bar on center of popcorn bag. Write "Happy Birthday" on bar with decorating icing. Press kettle corn onto top of cake. Store loosely covered.

1 Serving (Cake and Frosting Only): Calories 410; Total Fat 17g (Saturated Fat 3.5g, Trans Fat 3.5g); Cholesterol 40mg; Sodium 320mg; Total Carbohydrate 62g (Dietary Fiber 0g); Protein 1g **Exchanges:** ½ Starch, 3½ Other Carbohydrate, 3½ Fat **Carbohydrate Choices:** 4

Tip You can purchase already-popped kettle corn instead of popping microwave popcorn.

Cutting and Assembling Poppin' Up Happy Birthday Cake

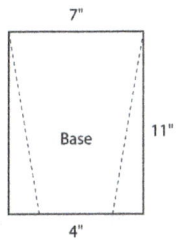

1. Cut 11 x 7-inch cake for popcorn box.

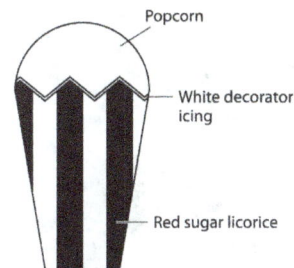

2. Arrange cake pieces on tray and decorate.

Gum Ball Machine Cake

Prep Time: 25 Minutes • **Start to Finish:** 3 Hours 10 Minutes • Makes 16 servings

Birthday cakes CAN be easy! There are no special decorating skills required for this one—candies and frosting create the fun.

1 Heat oven to 350°F (325°F for dark or nonstick pans). Grease bottoms only of 1 (8-inch or 9-inch) round cake pan and 1 (8-inch) square cake pan.

2 In large bowl, beat cake mix, soda pop, oil, egg whites and a few drops food color with electric mixer on low speed 30 seconds, then on medium speed 2 minutes, scraping bowl occasionally. Divide batter evenly between pans.

3 Bake 26 to 34 minutes or until toothpick inserted in center comes out clean (times may vary between the two pans). Cool 10 minutes; remove from pans to cooling rack. Cool completely, about 1 hour. Freeze cakes uncovered about 1 hour for easier frosting.

4 Place round cake near one end of tray for globe of gum ball machine; frost top and side with half of the frosting. Place square cake next to round cake for machine base. Stir 1 teaspoon food color into remaining frosting; frost sides and top of base with frosting. Wrap candy bar with foil. Place foil-wrapped candy bar near bottom of base. Use decorating gel to draw trap door on candy bar. Arrange chocolate coin and peanut candy above candy bar. Arrange gum balls on globe. Store loosely covered.

Cake

1 box Betty Crocker SuperMoist white cake mix

1¼ cups bubble gum–flavored soda pop or water

⅓ cup vegetable oil

3 egg whites

Red or blue food color (to match color of soda pop), if desired

Tray or cardboard (24 x 16), covered with foil or wrapping paper and plastic food wrap

Frosting and Decorations

1 container (12 oz) Betty Crocker Whipped vanilla frosting

1 teaspoon red or blue liquid or paste food color

1 bar (1.5 oz) chocolate-covered crispy candy

1 tube (0.68 oz) blue decorating gel

1 foil-covered chocolate coin

1 peanut-shaped candy

Gum balls

1 Serving: Calories 260; Total Fat 10g (Saturated Fat 2.5g, Trans Fat 1.5g); Cholesterol 0mg; Sodium 230mg; Total Carbohydrate 39g (Dietary Fiber 0g); Protein 2g **Exchanges:** ½ Starch, 2 Other Carbohydrate, 2 Fat **Carbohydrate Choices:** 2½

Tip If you don't have a candy bar to use for the trap door, you can use decorating icing or gel to draw it on the cake.

Just for Fun

"Let's Party" Cake

Prep Time: 30 Minutes • **Start to Finish:** 1 Hour 45 Minutes • Makes 12 servings

1 box Betty Crocker SuperMoist yellow cake mix (or any other flavor)

Water, vegetable oil and eggs called for on cake mix box

1 container (12 oz or 1 lb) Betty Crocker Whipped fluffy white frosting or Rich & Creamy vanilla frosting

Yellow and red food colors

Blue and green neon food colors

3 packages (2.17 oz each) tropical flavor candy-coated fruit-flavored chewy candies or 1 bag (8 oz) candy-coated chocolate candies

Stack up some delicious fun with a birthday cake that's super easy to make. And because part of it is cupcakes, it's extra fun to eat!

1 Heat oven to 350°F (325°F for dark or nonstick pans). Grease and flour bottom and side of 9-inch round cake pan, or spray with baking spray with flour. Place paper baking cup in each of 12 regular-size muffin cups.

2 Make cake batter as directed on box. Pour half of batter in round pan; divide remaining batter evenly among muffin cups. Bake as directed on box. Cool completely, about 1 hour.

3 In small bowl, place 1 tablespoon of the frosting; stir in 2 drops yellow food color. In another small bowl, place ¼ cup of the frosting, 3 drops yellow food color and 1 drop red food color; stir to make orange frosting. In third small bowl, place ½ cup of the frosting; stir in 7 drops blue neon food color. To remaining frosting in container, stir in 7 drops green neon food color.

4 Trim off rounded top of cake layer; place on serving plate cut side down. Frost top and side with green frosting. Frost 7 cupcakes with blue frosting, 4 cupcakes with orange frosting and 1 cupcake with yellow frosting. Place 1 blue cupcake on center of green frosted cake. Place remaining blue cupcakes, sides touching, in circle around center cupcake. Place 2 rows of 2 orange cupcakes on top center of blue cupcakes. Place yellow cupcake on top center of orange cupcakes. Press candies into frosting to decorate. Store loosely covered at room temperature.

1 Serving: Calories 420; Total Fat 18g (Saturated Fat 4.5g, Trans Fat 2g); Cholesterol 55mg; Sodium 310mg; Total Carbohydrate 61g (Dietary Fiber 0g); Protein 2g **Exchanges:** 1 Starch, 3 Other Carbohydrate, 3½ Fat **Carbohydrate Choices:** 4

Tip You can freeze the unfrosted cake and cupcakes (tightly covered) for up to 2 months.

Spiral Candle Cake

Prep Time: 20 Minutes • **Start to Finish:** 2 Hours 8 Minutes • Makes 16 servings

Go ahead and celebrate! Dazzle birthday celebrants with a fun and clever candle decorating idea, not to mention a moist and delicious cake!

1 Heat oven to 350°F (325°F for dark or nonstick pans). Make, bake and cool cake as directed on box for 2 (8-inch or 9-inch) rounds.

2 While cake is cooling, place candles in warm water until soft and pliable; wrap each candle around pencil. Cool candles about 15 seconds; remove pencils.

3 Place 1 cake layer rounded side down on serving plate. Spread with about ⅓ cup of the frosting. Top with second layer, rounded side up. Frost side and top of cake with remaining frosting. Arrange candles and wafers on cake.

1 box Betty Crocker SuperMoist cake mix (any flavor)

Water, vegetable oil and eggs called for on cake mix box

Thin sparkler candles, 6½ x ⅛ inch

Pencils

1 container (1 lb or 12 oz) Betty Crocker Rich & Creamy or Whipped frosting (any flavor)

Flat mint or rainbow candy-coating wafers, as desired

1 Serving: Calories 290; Total Fat 13g (Saturated Fat 3g, Trans Fat 1.5g); Cholesterol 40mg; Sodium 260mg; Total Carbohydrate 41g (Dietary Fiber 0g); Protein 1g **Exchanges:** ½ Starch, 2 Other Carbohydrate, 2½ Fat **Carbohydrate Choices:** 3

Tip The back of a tablespoon or serving spoon works well for swirling the frosting onto a cake.

Trix Cereal Crunch Cake

Prep Time: 20 Minutes • **Start to Finish:** 1 Hour 20 Minutes • Makes 12 servings

1 box Betty Crocker SuperMoist white cake mix

Water, vegetable oil and egg whites called for on cake mix box

Yellow, red, neon green and neon blue liquid food colors

2 teaspoons grated orange peel

2 teaspoons grated lime peel

1 container (12 oz) Betty Crocker Whipped fluffy white frosting

½ cup Trix cereal

Kids will love this bright-colored cake with Trix cereal!

1 Heat oven to 350°F (325°F for dark or nonstick pans). Grease bottoms only of 2 (8- or 9-inch) round cake pans. Make cake batter as directed on box.

2 Divide cake batter evenly between two separate medium bowls (about 2 cups each). In one bowl, add 25 drops yellow food color and 4 drops red food color; mix well. Stir in orange peel. Pour into one of the pans. In other bowl, add 25 drops neon green food color and 2 drops neon blue food color; mix well. Stir in lime peel. Pour into other pan.

3 Bake and cool cake as directed on box for 8- or 9-inch rounds.

4 Place green cake layer top side down on serving plate. Spread ⅓ cup of the frosting on top. Top with orange cake layer, top side up. Frost side and top of cake with remaining frosting. Sprinkle with cereal.

1 Serving: Calories 330; Total Fat 14g (Saturated Fat 3.5g, Trans Fat 2g); Cholesterol 0mg; Sodium 320mg; Total Carbohydrate 50g (Dietary Fiber 0g); Protein 2g **Exchanges:** 1 Starch, 2½ Other Carbohydrate, 2½ Fat **Carbohydrate Choices:** 3

Tip Neon food color gives the brightest color, but you can substitute regular food color if you don't have the neon.

Butterfly Cake

Prep Time: 40 Minutes • **Start to Finish:** 3 Hours 35 Minutes • Makes 8 servings

Cake

1 box Betty Crocker SuperMoist yellow cake mix

Water, vegetable oil and eggs called for on cake mix box

Tray or cardboard (10 x 10 inches), covered with wrapping paper and plastic food wrap or foil

Frosting and Decorations

1 container (1 lb) Betty Crocker Rich & Creamy vanilla frosting

1 candy stick (8 to 10 inches long)

Food color (in desired colors)

Decorating gel (from 0.68-oz tube) in any color

Decorating sugar crystals (any color)

8 jelly beans or candy-coated almonds

Small round candy decorations

This pretty cake is perfect for a group of youngsters that enjoy being out of doors. The cake can be decorated with any variety of colors and you can use paper on the tray to match your theme.

1 Heat oven to 350°F (325°F for dark or nonstick pans). Grease or spray bottoms and sides of 2 (8- or 9-inch) round cake pans. Make, bake and cool cake as directed on box for 8- or 9-inch rounds. Wrap and freeze 1 layer for later use. Freeze remaining layer 45 minutes before cutting to reduce crumbs.

2 Cut off rounded top of cake to make flat surface; place cake cut side down on work surface. Cut cake in half crosswise; cut each half into one-third and two-third pieces as shown in diagram 1). Place cake pieces on platter to form butterfly as shown in diagram 2. Gently separate cake pieces to form wings as shown in diagram 3.

3 Reserve ½ cup frosting in small bowl; set aside. Spread top and sides of cake with thin layer of frosting to seal in crumbs. Refrigerate or freeze cake 30 to 60 minutes to set frosting. Frost with remaining frosting. Place candy stick between cake pieces for butterfly body.

4 Stir food color into reserved frosting until well blended. Spread over cake in desired pattern on wings. Outline wing patterns with gel. Sprinkle with sugar crystals. Place jelly beans on corners of wings. Decorate butterfly with candy decorations. Store loosely covered.

1 Serving (Cake and Frosting Only): Calories 400; Total Fat 17g (Saturated Fat 3.5g, Trans Fat 3.5g); Cholesterol 40mg; Sodium 320mg; Total Carbohydrate 60g (Dietary Fiber 0g); Protein 1g **Exchanges:** ½ Starch, 3½ Other Carbohydrate, 3½ Fat **Carbohydrate Choices:** 4

Tip Turn the leftover cake layer into a trifle! Cut it into 1-inch cubes, and layer them with chocolate pudding and fresh strawberries in a large glass bowl. Top with whipped cream.

Cutting and Assembling Butterfly Cake

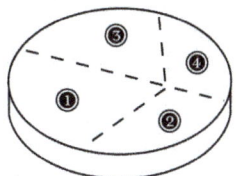

1. Cut cake for wings.

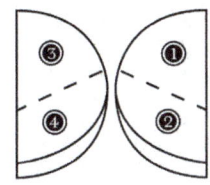

2. Arrange pieces on tray to form butterfly.

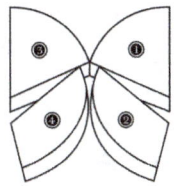

3. Separate pieces to form wings.

Just for Fun

Confetti Birthday Cake

Prep Time: 20 Minutes • **Start to Finish:** 2 Hours • Makes 16 servings

1 box Betty Crocker SuperMoist white cake mix

Water, vegetable oil and egg whites called for on cake mix box

1 bottle (1.75 oz) rainbow mix candy sprinkles

1 container (1 lb) Betty Crocker Rich & Creamy vanilla frosting

2 to 4 different colors decorating icing (in 4.25-oz tubes)

Any birthday party will be a hit with this pretty and appealing cake. Use your child's favorite colors to decorate it.

1 Heat oven to 350°F (325°F for dark or nonstick pans). Grease bottoms only of 2 (8-inch or 9-inch) round cake pans (do not spray with cooking spray).

2 Make cake batter as directed on box. Reserve 1 tablespoon candy sprinkles for decoration. Stir remaining sprinkles into batter. Divide batter evenly between pans.

3 Bake as directed on box for 8-inch or 9-inch rounds. Cool 10 minutes; remove from pans to cooling racks. Cool completely, about 1 hour.

4 Place 1 cake layer rounded side down on serving plate. Spread with ⅓ cup of the frosting. Top with second layer, rounded side up. Frost side and top of cake with remaining frosting.

5 Decorate top edge of cake with decorating icing in random squiggly pattern, overlapping colors. Sprinkle reserved candy sprinkles over top of cake. Store loosely covered.

1 Serving: Calories 340; Total Fat 13g (Saturated Fat 2g, Trans Fat 1.5g); Cholesterol 0mg; Sodium 280mg; Total Carbohydrate 54g (Dietary Fiber 0g); Protein 2g **Exchanges:** 1 Starch, 2½ Other Carbohydrate, 2½ Fat **Carbohydrate Choices:** 3½

Tip Enclose a sprinkle of brightly colored confetti in your party invitation. Then when you have the birthday party, scatter the same confetti on your dining or serving table, too.

Rainbow Angel Cake

Prep Time: 20 Minutes • **Start to Finish:** 3 Hours 10 Minutes • Makes 12 servings

1 box Betty Crocker white angel food cake mix

1¼ cups cold water

1 teaspoon grated lemon or orange peel

Red, yellow and green liquid food colors

1 cup Betty Crocker Rich & Creamy vanilla frosting (from 1-lb container)

12 to 15 square candy fruit chews

Simple food colors and candies create the wow for an easy-to-make cake that's perfect for any birthday party.

1 Move oven rack to lowest position (remove other racks). Heat oven to 350°F. In extra-large glass or metal bowl, beat cake mix, water and lemon peel with electric mixer on low speed 30 seconds; beat on medium speed 1 minute.

2 Divide batter evenly among 3 bowls. Gently stir 6 to 8 drops of one food color into each of the batters. Pour red batter into ungreased 10-inch angel food (tube) cake pan. (Do not use fluted tube cake pan or 9-inch angel food pan or batter will overflow.) Spoon yellow batter over red batter. Spoon green batter over yellow batter.

3 Bake 37 to 47 minutes or until top is dark golden brown and cracks feel very dry and not sticky. Do not underbake. Immediately turn pan upside down onto heatproof bottle or funnel until cake is completely cool, about 2 hours. Run knife around edges of cake; remove from pan to serving plate.

4 Spoon ½ cup of the frosting into microwavable bowl. Microwave uncovered on High about 15 seconds or until frosting can be stirred smooth and is thin enough to drizzle. (Or spoon frosting into 1-quart saucepan and heat over low heat, stirring constantly, until thin enough to drizzle.) Drizzle over cake.

5 Place remaining frosting in decorating bag with writing tip. Pipe a ribbon and bow on each candy square to look like a wrapped package. Arrange packages on top of cake. Store loosely covered at room temperature.

1 Serving (Cake and Frosting): Calories 240; Total Fat 5g (Saturated Fat 2g, Trans Fat 0g); Cholesterol 0mg; Sodium 370mg; Total Carbohydrate 45g (Dietary Fiber 0g); Protein 3g **Exchanges:** 1 Starch, 2 Other Carbohydrate, 1 Fat **Carbohydrate Choices:** 3

Tip Top this pretty cake with colorful candy packages instead of the white ones. Just add food color to the white frosting until it's the color you want.

Chocolate Lover's Dream Cake

Prep Time: 20 Minutes • **Start to Finish:** 3 Hours 35 Minutes • Makes 16 servings

Cake
- 1 box Betty Crocker SuperMoist chocolate fudge cake mix
- ¾ cup chocolate milk
- ⅓ cup butter or margarine, melted
- 3 eggs
- 1 container (8 oz) sour cream
- 1 box (4-serving size) chocolate fudge instant pudding and pie filling mix
- 1 bag (12 oz) semisweet chocolate chips (2 cups)

Glaze
- 1 cup semisweet chocolate chips (6 oz)
- ⅔ cup whipping cream

Toppings
- 1½ cups semisweet chocolate chips (9 oz)
- ½ cup caramel topping
- ½ cup toffee bits
- 1 bar (2.07 oz) milk chocolate–covered peanut, caramel and nougat candy, unwrapped, chopped

Chock-full of chocolate chips, this pretty cake is a chocolate lover's dream!

1 Heat oven to 350°F (325°F for dark or nonstick pan). Generously grease 12-cup fluted tube cake pan with shortening and lightly flour, or spray with baking spray with flour.

2 In large bowl, mix cake mix, chocolate milk, butter, eggs, sour cream and dry pudding mix with spoon until well blended (batter will be very thick). Stir in 2 cups chocolate chips. Spoon into pan.

3 Bake 56 to 64 minutes or until top springs back when touched lightly in center. Cool 10 minutes. Turn pan upside down onto cooling rack or heatproof serving plate; remove pan. Cool completely, about 2 hours.

4 Place 1 cup chocolate chips in small heatproof bowl. In 1-quart saucepan, heat whipping cream to simmering; pour over chips. Let stand 5 minutes; stir until smooth. Drizzle glaze over cake. Sprinkle with 1½ cups chocolate chips. Drizzle caramel topping over cake. Sprinkle with toffee bits and chopped candy. Store loosely covered at room temperature.

1 Serving: Calories 580; Total Fat 30g (Saturated Fat 17g, Trans Fat 0g); Cholesterol 70mg; Sodium 440mg; Total Carbohydrate 73g (Dietary Fiber 4g); Protein 6g **Exchanges:** 2 Starch, 3 Other Carbohydrate, 5½ Fat **Carbohydrate Choices:** 5

Tip For a milder chocolate flavor, substitute milk chocolate chips for the semisweet chips.

Metric Conversion Guide

Volume

U.S. Units	Canadian Metric	Australian Metric
¼ teaspoon	1 mL	1 ml
½ teaspoon	2 mL	2 ml
1 teaspoon	5 mL	5 ml
1 tablespoon	15 mL	20 ml
¼ cup	50 mL	60 ml
⅓ cup	75 mL	80 ml
½ cup	125 mL	125 ml
⅔ cup	150 mL	170 ml
¾ cup	175 mL	190 ml
1 cup	250 mL	250 ml
1 quart	1 liter	1 liter
1½ quarts	1.5 liters	1.5 liters
2 quarts	2 liters	2 liters
2½ quarts	2.5 liters	2.5 liters
3 quarts	3 liters	3 liters
4 quarts	4 liters	4 liters

Weight

U.S. Units	Canadian Metric	Australian Metric
1 ounce	30 grams	30 grams
2 ounces	55 grams	60 grams
3 ounces	85 grams	90 grams
4 ounces (¼ pound)	115 grams	125 grams
8 ounces (½ pound)	225 grams	225 grams
16 ounces (1 pound)	455 grams	500 grams
1 pound	455 grams	0.5 kilogram

Note: The recipes in this cookbook have not been developed or tested using metric measures. When converting recipes to metric, some variations in quality may be noted.

Measurements

Inches	Centimeters
1	2.5
2	5.0
3	7.5
4	10.0
5	12.5
6	15.0
7	17.5
8	20.5
9	23.0
10	25.5
11	28.0
12	30.5
13	33.0

Temperatures

Fahrenheit	Celsius
32°	0°
212°	100°
250°	120°
275°	140°
300°	150°
325°	160°
350°	180°
375°	190°
400°	200°
425°	220°
450°	230°
475°	240°
500°	260°

Recipe Testing and Calculating Nutrition Information

Recipe Testing:

- Large eggs and 2% milk were used unless otherwise indicated.
- Fat-free, low-fat, low-sodium or lite products were not used unless indicated.
- No nonstick cookware and bakeware were used unless otherwise indicated. No dark-colored, black or insulated bakeware was used.
- When a pan is specified, a metal pan was used; a baking dish or pie plate means ovenproof glass was used.
- An electric hand mixer was used for mixing only when mixer speeds are specified.

Calculating Nutrition:

- The first ingredient was used wherever a choice is given, such as ⅓ cup sour cream or plain yogurt.
- The first amount was used wherever a range is given, such as 3- to 3½-pound whole chicken.
- The first serving number was used wherever a range is given, such as 4 to 6 servings.
- "If desired" ingredients were not included.
- Only the amount of a marinade or frying oil that is absorbed was included.

America's most trusted cookbook is better than ever!

- 1,100 all-new photos, including hundreds of step-by-step images
- More than 1,500 recipes, with hundreds of inspiring variations and creative "mini" recipes for easy cooking ideas
- Brand-new features
- Gorgeous new design

Get the best edition of the *Betty Crocker Cookbook* today!

www.ingramcontent.com/pod-product-compliance
Lightning Source LLC
Chambersburg PA
CBHW071417290426
44108CB00014B/1861